Standing in the Gap

CORWIN CONNECTED EDUCATORS SERIES

Worlds of Making: Best Practices for Establishing a Makerspace for Your School
By Laura Fleming @NMHS_lms

Personalized Learning Plans for Teachers
By Tom Murray @thomascmurray and Jeff Zoul @Jeff_Zoul

Empowered Schools, Empowered Students: Creating Connected and Invested Learners
By Pernille Ripp @pernilleripp

Blogging for Educators: Tips for Getting Connected
By Starr Sackstein @mssackstein

Principal PD
By Joseph Sanfelippo @Joesanfelippofc and Tony Sinanis @TonySinanis

The Power of Branding: Telling Your School's Story
By Tony Sinanis @TonySinanis and Joseph Sanfelippo @Joesanfelippofc

The Educator's Guide to Creating Connections
Edited by Tom Whitby @tomwhitby

The Relevant Educator: How Connectedness Empowers Learning
By Tom Whitby @tomwhitby and Steven W. Anderson @web20classroom

Standing in the Gap

Empowering New Teachers
Through Connected Resources

Lisa Dabbs

Nicol R. Howard

CORWIN
A SAGE Company

FOR INFORMATION:

Corwin

A SAGE Company

2455 Teller Road

Thousand Oaks, California 91320

(800) 233–9936

www.corwin.com

SAGE Publications Ltd.

1 Oliver's Yard

55 City Road

London EC1Y 1SP

United Kingdom

SAGE Publications India Pvt. Ltd.

B 1/I 1 Mohan Cooperative Industrial Area

Mathura Road, New Delhi 110 044

India

SAGE Publications Asia-Pacific Pte. Ltd.

3 Church Street

#10–04 Samsung Hub

Singapore 049483

Printed in the United States of America

ISBN 978-1-4833-9139-7

This book is printed on acid-free paper.

Acquisitions Editor: Ariel Price

Editorial Assistant: Andrew Olson

Production Editor: Amy Joy Schroller

Copy Editor: Lana Todorovic-Arndt

Typesetter: C&M Digitals (P) Ltd.

Proofreader: Rae-Ann Goodwin

Cover and Interior Designer: Janet Kiesel

Marketing Manager: Lisa Lysne

Certified Chain of Custody
Promoting Sustainable Forestry
www.sfiprogram.org
SFI-01268

SFI label applies to text stock

15 16 17 18 19 10 9 8 7 6 5 4 3 2 1

Contents

Preface

My best friend is a high school math teacher. When I started working on the Corwin Connected Educators series, I excitedly told her about the power of using social media to connect with other educators. I passed on what I learned from the authors in this series: that the greatest resource educators have is each other. At a conference, she heard Jennie Magiera speak and finally made the leap to getting on Twitter. Although I wasn't sure she would continue tweeting, she did, and even joined Twitter chats like #connectedtl and #slowmathchat. A few days later, she texted me saying, "I seriously cannot thank you enough. You have changed my life."

Being "connected" seems deceptively simple: Just get on Twitter, right? But that's really not enough. For those who truly embrace connectedness, it's a lifestyle change, an openness to sharing and learning in an entirely new environment. We're seeing the impact of this shift in mindset worldwide. Policies are changing, new jobs in education are being created, hitherto impossible collaborations are happening, pedagogy is evolving, and there's a heightened awareness of each person's individual impact. All of these changes are explored in the Connected Educators series.

While you can see the full list of books on the series page, we're introducing several new books to the series; they will be published in the fall of 2015 and spring of 2016. These books each contribute something unique and necessary not only for educators who are new to the world of connected education, but also for those who have been immersed in it for some time.

Tom Whitby, coauthor of *The Relevant Educator,* has brought together a group of experienced connected educators in his new book, *The Educator's Guide to Creating Connections.* Contributors Pam Moran, George Couros, Kyle Pace, Adam Bellow, Lisa Nielsen, Kristen Swanson, Steven Anderson, and Shannon McClintock Miller discuss the ways that connectedness has impacted them and the benefits it can have for all educators—policy makers, school and district leaders, and teachers.

While all connected educators are evangelists for being connected, connectedness does not necessarily prevent common problems, such as isolation in leadership. In *Breaking Out of Isolation,* Spike Cook, Jessica Johnson, and Theresa Stager explain how connectedness can alleviate the loneliness leaders can feel in their position and also, when used effectively, help leaders maintain balance in their lives and stay motivated.

For districts and schools embracing the connected mindset and empowering all of their learners to use technology, a solid plan for digital citizenship is a must. In *Digital Citizenship,* Susan Bearden provides a look at how leaders can prepare teachers and students for the new responsibilities of using technology and interacting with others on a truly global platform.

Connected education provides unique opportunities for teachers in their classrooms as well. In *Standing in the Gap,* Lisa Dabbs and Nicol Howard explore the ways that social media can specifically help new teachers find resources, connect to mentors, and encourage each other in their careers. Erin Klein, Tom Murray, A. J. Juliani, and Ben Gilpin show how teachers can purposefully integrate technology and empower their students in both physical and digital classrooms in *Redesigning Learning Spaces.*

One of the most powerful impacts connected education can have is in reaching marginalized populations. In *Confident Voices,* John Spencer shows how social media and other technology tools can empower English language learners. Billy Krakower and Sharon LePage Plante have also discovered that technology can reach special and gifted learners as well.

The books in the Corwin Connected Educators series are supported by a companion website featuring videos, articles, downloadable forms, and other resources to help you as you start and continue your journey. Best of all, the authors in the series want to connect with *you!* We've provided their Twitter handles and other contact information on the companion website.

Once you've taken the step to joining a network, don't stop there. Share what you're doing; you never know when it will help someone else!

—*Peter DeWitt, Series Editor*
@PeterMDeWitt

—*Ariel Price, Associate Editor*
@arielkprice

Acknowledgments

We are thankful for this process and appreciate the opportunity to author this book in the Connected Educators series. Ariel Price and Peter DeWitt provided stellar support and feedback throughout this journey, and for that we are grateful.

We are two authors who came together, from different backgrounds, both with a desire to *stand in the gap* for new teachers. We realized along the way that even the most seasoned teacher may need someone to stand in support of them too.

Special thanks to our contributors—Scott Bedley, Elle Deyamport, Layla Wiedrick Henry, Betina Hsieh, Jamie Pesanti, and Bill Selak.

Thanks to all of the Connected Educators authors who paved the way by sharing their passions and stories unapologetically.

About the Authors

Lisa Dabbs is an educational consultant, blogger, and speaker. Lisa began her career as an elementary school teacher in Southern California. During that time, she assisted in writing a federal grant project and became the project director of a language and literacy program. She managed that program, reporting on a regular basis to OBEMLA (now OELA—Office of English Language Acquisition) and successfully guided it through 5 years of completion. Her passion to serve as a leader soon moved her to apply for a principalship. She did so and spent 14 years as an elementary school principal in four Los Angeles County school districts. In time she was selected to work as a coach/consultant for Kaplan K–12 Educational Corporation as a middle school consultant and ELA coach in Los Angeles Unified School District. She provided staff and teachers with professional development, technology support, and classroom coaching. Lisa is an adjunct professor at the University of La Verne and has taught graduate level courses in School Administration for Concordia University, Irvine.

Lisa has a B.A. in child development, an M.Ed. in educational administration from the University of La Verne, Life Multiple Subjects Credential, Bilingual Certificate of Competency, and Administrative Credential. Lisa is active in social media, and with her passion to support and mentor new teachers, she created and founded New Teacher Chat #ntchat. The chat is a vibrant, weekly, education discussion group on Twitter and is practitioner focused and supportive. New, preservice, and experienced teachers join her weekly on the chat to discuss topics germane to the needs of the new practitioner. A Facebook page, Google Plus community, and Remind.com class that she moderates add additional ways to connect.

Lisa is a resident blogger at Edutopia.org and has served as a member of their social media marketing team. She also served for 4 years as the facilitator of Edutopia's New Teacher Connections group. Lisa has served as a curriculum developer for Edupad.com and currently is part of the social media team at iThinkWrite.com. Lisa has also written for the Huffington Post, Smartblogs, Kids Discover, and The Teacher's Lounge. She also moderates Women in EdTech on Google Plus.

Lisa is a regular commentator at the BAM! Radio Network where she discusses leadership and educational issues. She is also a big #edcamp fan and is on the organizing team for @edcampLA and @edcampLDR and was one of the founding members of the first edcamp in California. Lisa is also a comoderator of California Edchat #caedchat.

Lisa has presented at local, statewide, and national education conferences including the 140 Character Conference in Los Angeles on Social Media, Computer Using Educators (CUE), San Diego Computer Using Educators (SDCUE), California Council on Teacher Education (CCTE), Orange County Reading Association (OCRA), Association of Supervision and Curriculum Development (ASCD), and International Society of Technology Educators (ISTE). She also frequently presents webinars for Simple K12, Edweb, Follett, Laura Candler, McGraw Hill, Reform Symposium, and Classroom 2.0 Live. She is active in her community having served as a library board trustee and currently as the vice president of an award-winning literacy nonprofit in her town. You can find her blogging and sharing her passion to support and mentor new teachers at LisaDabbs.com and on Twitter @teachwithsoul.

Nicol R. Howard, Ph.D., has had the pleasure of serving as an educator in various capacities over the past years 12 years. She has taught at the high school level (ninth to twelfth grades and special education) in the Compton Unified School District and Grades K through 4 in the Corona-Norco Unified District and the Santa Ana Unified School District (SAUSD). Nicol is currently the program specialist in personalized/blended learning within the Learning Innovation with Technology department at SAUSD. She is also an adjunct professor at Chapman University, where she obtained her doctorate and received the prestigious 2015 James L. Doti Outstanding Graduate Student Award (university level) and the 2015 Distinguished Ph.D. in Education Outstanding Student Award (college level). In higher education, Nicol has facilitated multiple courses in teacher education related to technology, learning theories, and research methods. Her personal research interests are in the effective use of technology in K–12 education and equity issues related to academic success in STEM Education and career trajectories.

Nicol earned her B.A. at the University of California at Los Angeles (UCLA), her M.A. in Educational Technology at Azusa Pacific University, and her Ph.D. in education at Chapman University. Her past and present experiences, along with the notion of equity in education (specifically achievement), influence her commitment as an educator, researcher, tech enthusiast, learner, and educational writer. Nicol's concern for certain inequities in education and her research projects have led to publications in educational journals, such as the *EDUCAUSE Review* and the *Urban Education Journal*. Additionally, she has written for Edutopia and Corwin Connect.

Nicol's overall commitment to the field of education has led her to speak at various national and international conferences, such as the Annual Conferences for the American Educational Research Association (AERA), California Council on Teacher Education

(CCTE), Emerging Scholars Conference (ESC), the Diversity Conference, Computer Using Educators (CUE), and San Diego Computer Using Educators (SDCUE). She has also been invited to guest moderate for #teacheredchat and #profchat on Twitter @nicolrhoward. Please visit http://www.NicolHoward.com to learn more about Dr. Nicol R. Howard.

To my husband Randy for his love and tremendous support to me in this journey, to Jason and Aaron who make me a proud Momma and to my Grandma Mima who is the inspiration for my work! To my friends who supported me to bring the vision that I had to author a book to stand in the gap for new teacher practitioners worldwide, based on the foundations of New Teacher Chat!

—Lisa

Thank you to my husband, Keith, and children Micaela and Kamau for the loving nudges, the encouragement, and the support to do this work. The work I do calls for boldly standing in the gap to support K–12 educators and teacher educators who share my same vision to positively influence the acceleration of student achievement for all.

—Nicol

Introduction

With the wide array of social media tools and professional learning communities available, there is no reason for new teachers to feel alone, isolated, disconnected, or at a loss for knowing what to do in any situation. Every year, schools in the United States hire more than 200,000 new teachers for that first day of class. As summer rolls around, at least 22,000 have quit. Even those who make it beyond the first year aren't likely to stay long: about 30 percent of new teachers leave the profession after just 3 years, and more than 45 percent after 5. Does all of this sound scary? What can we do to support new teachers better? How can we support and help make connections to bridge the gap between what new teachers already know from preservice programs to their current practice?

All teachers need a support system, especially those in the beginning years of service. Research shows that there is a tremendous need for new teachers to receive the opportunity of mentoring in order to be successful in their work. Faced with too much fear, or the perception that others cannot be trusted, new teachers are apprehensive about reaching out to try new things. Teaching is a complex and challenging profession these days, but the power of being connected to other teachers is paramount to success. Through easy-to-implement strategies, this book will provide ways for new teachers to build confidence in harnessing the power of social media to connect to resources and those in the field who can stand in the gap to support them.

Chapter 1 focuses on the importance of teachers making connections to online communities. With the upsurge of social media use in education, this is a timely and relevant chapter that provides a practical approach to making connections for the purpose of professional development and/or locating teaching and learning resources. Chapter 2 extends the idea of connecting beyond the realm of familiar people. This chapter challenges new teachers to not only make their own local and global connections, but to consider their students by connecting them to other classrooms around the world. Chapter 3 is all about the different ways to connect to resources, and your students, when building your classroom. A classroom built only by the teacher is only for the teacher. In Chapter 4, we offer practical steps for making connections to plan your lessons. You are not on an island, so it is often helpful to use online resources and connect with other teachers when lesson planning. As we move into Chapter 5, we begin to discuss the various ways to communicate with students and parents using Web-based tools and/or social media. Finally in Chapter 6, we outline steps for connecting to and utilizing the power of a face-to-face and/or virtual mentor.

> A classroom built only by the teacher is only for the teacher.

Each chapter includes a practical guide, called "Put It in Practice" (PiP), to support the implementation of key strategies for connecting to resources. After the PiPs, there are suggested "Action Steps" for new teachers to follow as they build and strengthen their connections. This book will serve as a guide to help both new teachers, and anyone working with new teachers, to mobilize the power of connected resources to mentor and empower new teachers to make informed decisions, create meaningful lesson plans, and connect to the most important stakeholders in education: the students!

Making Connections to Online Communities of Practice

Lisa Dabbs and Nicol R. Howard

As a new teacher, you may have noticed that there has been an upsurge of social media use taking place over the past decade. Groups throughout various sectors of the world, including educators, are increasingly bending toward the use of social media, attempting to reap the benefits of this modern technology. Businesses may turn to social media to establish brand identity and improve customer service. Institutes of higher learning may utilize social media to remain connected with prospective and current students, as well as alumni.

Social media seems to be a thriving enterprise and certainly seems to engage many people across the world. As we know that teacher quality (more specifically professional development) has been shown to be critical to student learning, there is a need for you to understand social media use through online communities of practice (CoP) for your professional learning. It's also important to be able to leverage social media as you grow in your practice.

Time is limited! How can you find that needle in a haystack lesson that will impact your students positively? Certain social media offer an interesting platform for teachers to engage in online professional development, as the constraints of time and locale are minimized. Ok, so you're heading off to that required professional development (PD) session after school or on your staff meeting day. Wouldn't you like a chance to select your own CoP and PD? Social media allows new teachers an opportunity to engage in social learning that is often specific to areas of interest for their professional growth and development.

> *Lisa: I'm an enthusiastic educator from a family of educators. My dad was a teacher, marching band director, and assistant principal. My mom was a teacher, and my uncle was a teacher and principal. But the one who was the most influential in my life was my grandmother.*
>
> *An immigrant from Mexico, born in the early 1900s, my grandmother was an avid reader, driven by a constant desire to seek out her own learning. She attended University of California, Los Angeles (UCLA), graduated summa cum laude, and became a high school language teacher. Fluent in five languages, she also became an adjunct professor. She was convinced that through the power of education, people could rise above poverty and achieve their dreams. I also believe that to be true and she still inspires me daily.*
>
> *This foundation is what led me to become a teacher and eventually a school principal. It also led me to grow my technology interests and master all the apps and hardware tools that I could get a hold of. I implemented new tech in my schools and classrooms, and led initiatives to boost the tech infrastructure on my campuses. It wasn't until*

I left the structure of the school district, however that I discovered the world of social media. The power that it has to transform learning and connect me to educators around the world is unprecedented. I'm an active participant in online communities, webinars, conferences, and twitter chats that widen my learning lens and challenge my thinking. Sharing these same tools that will bring powerful educational transformations with others is my passion. It's what led me to found New Teacher Chat #ntchat on Twitter!

Nicol: I was born into a family that revels in the advancement of new technologies. By the age of 9, I already knew how to wire our TVs to cable through our VHS receiver. At age 15, I made recommendations for household technology purchases. Technology evolved and we entered the computer era. Soon my passion for learning new technology emerged, and I remember the first social network I joined—MySpace. The benefit for me in joining this online community was the fact that I could choose what information I wanted to disclose about myself. I did not have to be concerned with my caramel-colored skin misleading perceptions or driving first impressions about who I was. Years later, I now participate in online PD opportunities using Twitter with full disclosure (including a photo) about who I am. Although I now openly participate in online communities of practice, understanding the comfort in choosing to maintain one's anonymity informs my interest in exploring online CoPs in which individuals create their own profiles (with photos).

Lisa and Nicol: We vividly remember our first years of teaching, and those feelings of uncertainty as we sought to build a personal support system. With the wide array of social media tools and professional learning communities available, there is no longer a reason for new teachers to feel alone, isolated, or at a loss for knowing what to do in difficult situations. All teachers need a support system, especially in the first years of service.

PiP (Put It Into Practice) With Elvira Deyamport

Elvira Deyamport, Ed.S., is a connected educator who is passionate about sharing her love for technology integration with educators in her field. She teaches gifted students in Grades 2–6, where she incorporates tools like Skype, Blogger, Twitter, Edmodo, and various Apple applications. Her philosophy revolves around exposing and connecting her students to a variety of people, places, and authentic learning experiences. To read more about Elvira, visit her About Me Page at http://about.me/deyamportelvira or follow her on Twitter at @elle_gifted.

The biggest struggle I have faced in teaching is when I need ideas for my classroom. I used to spend endless hours searching on Google or Pinterest for lesson ideas and constantly get overwhelmed with the possibilities available. Many times, the resources I came across would either be too simple or too complex for my students. Throughout the years, I have learned how to narrow my search to focus on the *what,* but also the *who.*

Where to Start. When I am looking for my *what,* or my topic focus, my go-to places are Share My Lesson and ReadWriteThink. Both sites are free and offer a variety of hands-on and minds-on lessons that can easily be modified to fit the needs of my students. While ReadWriteThink emphasizes language arts, reading, and writing, Share My Lesson offers units, resources, and lessons across subject areas. Both include high-quality resources, such as graphic organizers and interactives that can complement almost any unit. They are worth taking a look at!

ACTION STEPS

Are you new to social media or the idea of using it for professional development? Are you ready to move beyond Facebook to connect

Share My Lesson: *http://www.sharemylesson.com/*

ReadWriteThink: *http://www.readwritethink.org/*

It's All About Connections. Although knowing our *what* is important, just as valuable is knowing our *whom*. Throughout the years, I have been active on Twitter and have connected with other educators in the field of gifted and elementary education. I have built relationships with certain colleagues, which has changed my Twitter experience from a place of retweets to a space for dialogue and collaboration. Now, if I have a question about a lesson or approach, I can send a tweet to my Personalized Learning Network (PLN) for feedback and recommendations. Instead of blindly favoring a tweet from my PLN, I now know that an educator I trust has vetted the resource. If I am in need of some inspiration for my classroom, I can take it a step further and schedule a Google Hangout with gifted educators to share exciting projects. Twitter has many opened doors for me and has allowed me to connect with educators who share similar passions and goals as me. If you are a teacher on Twitter, consider starting your own PLN—you will not regret it!

Staying Organized. As a connected educator, organization is key. You must consider a space to hold all of the wonderful resources and ideas you encounter. Although there are many platforms to house digital resources, my personal favorite has been Diigo. This site has the capacity to store bookmarks, notes, and even favorites saved on Twitter. In addition, you are able to follow other Diigo users and have access to their public bookmark lists. This tool has worked for me because it is simple and convenient. My best advice is to find a tool that works for you and stick with it.

Used with permission of Elvira Deyamport.

with educators in your online CoP? Are you excited to see how it can support you to become a connected educator? Let's look at some simple steps that you can use to prepare to make connections to your online CoP.

1. Build Your Social Media Bio

Before getting started with using a social media space to develop your online CoP or virtual professional learning experience, it is essential that you create your bio. As an active Twitter user, there's nothing worse than seeing that your new follower, who may have tweeted a great resource, only has his or her name and an "egg" (the default avatar for new accounts) in his or her Twitter bio. No one on Twitter wants to follow an "egg." Taking the time to develop and create a thoughtful bio with your name, your position, your passions and interests, makes for a much more interesting and engaging opportunity. You are also more likely to build a following of like-minded professionals in your same field. Don't stop with your Twitter profile—do the same for the other social media spaces you join. Step 1 is imperative when seeking out appropriate online CoP and virtual professional development opportunities. We've provided more resources on this topic on our companion site, located at http://www.corwin.com/connectededucators.

See the samples of our Twitter bios below, to help you get started.

Lisa Dabbs
@teachwithsoul
Consultant. Speaker. Blogger @edutopia. @CorwinPress Author!
Founder #NTchat Weds. 5pt/8et. Former Principal. Soc Media
@ithinkwrite. @edcampLA org. #mentor
California · about.me/lisamichelle

2. Choose Your Tool

Once you've got that great bio developed and prepared, decide which social media spaces are going to serve you best. Many educators use Facebook exclusively, but there are so many other tools

that offer a richer experience. Keep in mind that a user of one platform may not be the user of another; therefore, limiting yourself to one may eliminate a learning opportunity only available on another. We personally encourage educators new to this idea of using social media to connect to online communities of practice (or virtual professional development) to try Twitter, Google Plus, and Ning sites as they begin to consider their own professional learning needs. These spaces are all great access points for 24/7 learning and sharing. Let's briefly take a look at them:

- Twitter offers the opportunity for resource sharing by following hashtags and participating in chats. You can jump on Twitter, any time, any day and learn something new! A list of Twitter chats to consider joining are offered on the Corwin Connected Educators companion website.

- Google Plus has numerous free webinars via Google Hangouts that are also great ways to participate and learn.

- Ning sites are an excellent point of entry for those who might not be ready for the two listed above. A Ning is a community that has been set up for the purpose of connecting and collaborating. There are many on the Web that can be joined for free and will provide numerous learning opportunities. One of the most popular Ning communities for educators is Classroom 2.0.

- Instagram is another platform that offers opportunities to connect and share with other educators. You can search for relevant content by hashtags or images. You also have the ability to follow teachers or professional organizations that post content you have an interest in exploring further.

- Teachers Pay Teachers (TpT) is one of the best-kept secrets for building your community. It does not offer an environment conducive for an online dialogue; however, you may find that teachers who upload useful resources have an online presence established with other social media. TpT lets you peek into the window of someone's classroom. Seeing the happenings in a colleague's classroom is not something you will have many opportunities to do. So, take advantage of this resource, for the purpose of connecting with other teachers, and allow it to bring you closer to someone in your online learning community.

Finally, be sure to seek out and connect with colleagues who may already be in these spaces and using these tools. Would you rather show up to the party alone or with a friend? Do you remember the buddy system? This may be your same approach to joining new online CoP. After connecting with colleagues, have a look at their connections and decide if they may be following someone who you may also see as a member of your community of practice. This approach serves as somewhat of a vetting process for you as well. As a new user of social media for learning, this will save you time and frustration!

3. Recommended Practices

As you decide to begin this journey, we want to recommend the following:

- Find and use a mentor who has experience with social media and have him or her as your guide on the side.

- Choose a tool, get comfortable with it, practice with it, and use it often!

- Seek out free online professional development opportunities.
- Collaborate and share resources that you find with colleagues and encourage them to join you.

Don't be afraid to ask for help!

4. Attend Events

Attending events, such as virtual conferences or a webinar, is the final PiP step in preparing to make connections to online CoP. Here are a few we recommend:

- Simple K12
- Classroom 2.0
- Edweb
- Edweek
- ASCD

- Virtual Round Table
- McGraw-Hill
- Discovery
- Scholastic
- All4ed.org

As experienced social media users, we know that these four PiP steps will be supportive to you in the process of considering the use of social media to connect to CoP and virtual PDs. Not only do we hope that you will find these steps useful in supporting your practice, but we also hope that you will be excited about discovering new PD opportunities in the virtual world.

Making Connections Locally and Globally

Nicol R. Howard

How common is it to assume that connecting with peer educators will be a cinch? The first professional development day of the school year arrives, and you make a promise (to yourself) to connect with other teachers and/or your district curriculum specialists. You want to connect for the benefit of your students, yet you also know how important connecting can be when it pertains to staying motivated throughout the academic year. The first month flies by, back-to-school night passes, and you still haven't even peeked into your neighbor's classroom. No new teacher is alone in this experience; however, forgetting to talk to other teachers about teaching should be a problem of the past.

Starting out as a new teacher can be likened to an unknown exploration. New teachers should not be left to set sail into open water with no anchor or lifeline. Starting out as a new teacher with 20–120 young lives in your hands can appear to be a daunting task, if you are left to tackle the job alone. When given the charge to academically and socially prepare students for their next year of learning, teachers should also be given access to all of the resources that may potentially support their successful journey. However, what always seems to be missing is the push to connect with others locally and globally.

Advancements in technology now make it easier for teachers to connect with one another, so long gone are the days of using time as the excuse for not reaching out to one another. Educators not only use email to stay connected, but they also use other platforms, such as Skype, Google Hangout, Facebook, Pinterest, Instagram, Twitter, Edmodo, and Schoology. In addition to connecting and collaborating through online platforms, face-to-face opportunities are often provided by local district offices in the form of professional development meetings.

So, why is it so important to stay connected? In order to successfully create and maintain dynamic learning environments, teachers must be encouraged to make local and global connections. Encouragement can certainly be in the form of words, as well as mass e-mails related to local professional development opportunities. Additionally, districts should support new teachers by establishing relationships with other districts around the world. Teachers who are already making global connections will instantly appreciate the support from their district, and new teachers will potentially become just as enthusiastic about the possibilities to come from making new connections. The lessons learned and resources acquired through these connections can strengthen teachers personally and professionally, while widening their sphere of support and increasing access to resources for their students.

> The time of being limited to the four-walled area called a classroom is only by teacher decision now.
>
> —Scott Bedley

When I began teaching, peer-educators rarely connected beyond the district meetings that required everyone to be in attendance. "Let's chat tomorrow over lunch," "Sorry I can't meet today, I have papers to grade so I can leave early," and "Maybe next week" were common phrases heard throughout the halls. Time certainly seemed to be a factor when trying to arrange face-to-face meet-ups with colleagues. Although Twitter went live in 2006, few teachers I knew were considering it as a tool to connect beyond the classroom. Actually, very few were even checking e-mail regularly. I vividly recall my introduction to Twitter and my first Twitter chat in 2009. Through one chat, I met a teacher in Germany and a teacher in India. Both educators contributed to multiple projects and lessons taught over my next years of teaching.

In 2009, I launched my global learning project on energizing environments. The peer-educator I met from India participated in my project by allowing her classroom to connect and collaborate with mine, in the United States. Over the next 2 years, we stayed connected and established a blogging relationship between our classrooms. Naturally, our students raised many questions about the similarities and differences between our schools and cultures. I quickly learned how to successfully facilitate a meaningful dialogue between my students, while modeling how to make global connections. Making this connection actually encouraged my personal and professional growth. I learned an essential lesson about the importance of developing culturally relevant and sensitive projects.

ACTION STEPS

1. Stick With It

Scheduling a time to connect is the first step to making local and global connections with peer educators and other classrooms. Scheduling may begin with making a phone call to another teacher and setting a date to meet; however, the key is to stick with the scheduled meeting date. In other words, make certain you follow through with the plan. Do not make time a variable that interferes

(Action Steps continue on p. 20.)

PiP (Put It Into Practice) With Nicol Howard

Global learning projects (GLPs) present an innovative way of learning about your own culture, other cultures, and a little geography. GLPs consist of an online curriculum designed to be completed simultaneously by multiple classrooms around the world. Ideally classrooms connect with one another asynchronously through a blog, discussion board, or VoiceThread (voicethread.com). Or, they connect with one another synchronously through video conferencing tools (e.g., Skype) or live Twitter chats. Forget about the boring, linear lessons that require rote memorization. GLPs allow students and teachers to connect cross-culturally across the globe. Classrooms full of students learn about their own culture and community before connecting with another class to learn more about their culture. The students in both classes do not initially set out to learn about each other's culture or school customs, but eventually the organic conversations and/or blog exchanges take them down this path of discovery.

How it works. I begin with a little research to determine if there may be any interesting lesson topics my class has in common with students in a similar grade-level from another country. Ideally the lesson or unit you choose is one that is connected to a real-world issue. For example, one year we decided to learn more about environmental awareness. I wasn't sure if this topic would be of any interest to other classrooms, so I sent out a tweet to my Personalized Learning Network. Within minutes, I received a tweet back from a teacher in India who was interested in collaborating with my students and me on a GLP. Next I began writing the curriculum for our unit, and I used a free Web service to post the curriculum online (www.e2project4schools.com). After a few back and forth e-mails, my collaborating teacher and I decided on the date to start our lesson.

Unfortunately, the time difference did not allow for synchronous meetings; therefore, we used VoiceThread and a blog to communicate and share our ideas and findings with one another. My class was not only learning more about how to care for their own school environment, but they were learning how students in schools around the world care for their schools. I remember when my students finally had a chance to look at the photos of the students from the other school, in action. After developing a recycling plan for our school campus, my students were surprised to discover that students from our partner school in India were literally cleaning the school campus with soapy suds. My students also noticed that the students in India did not wear the same school uniforms that they wore, which led to a rich conversation about cultural attire. After whole-class conversations about the differences we learned about our classroom and the classroom in India, my students came up with a list of thoughtful questions to ask on the discussion board and blog.

More details . . . Although we initially set out to complete the unit in 1–2 weeks, the time difference between our countries required flexibility and patience. I had to wait up late some evenings for e-mail replies, but the end result was well worth it. I also had to remain flexible and willing to address the unexpected. I did not anticipate the magnitude or depth of the culture-related questions that my students would have or would be asked. Allowing time to research and answer these questions was essential.

Some advantages include the expansion of collaboration beyond the walls of your own classroom. Your students also have a chance to engage in real-world lessons, while learning about the ways other people around the world may respond to similar issues. I love that GLPs offer students a unique opportunity to collaborate, to think critically, and to revisit and revise their own solutions to real-world problems.

Scott teaches fifth grade, and he is an author and speaker. He was a 2014 Orange County Teacher of the Year, California State Teacher of the Year Finalist, and 2013 Project Tomorrow's Innovative STEM Teacher Award winner. He's the creator of Technology Applied Science Fair and co-host for The BedleyBros EdChat Show (#EdChat). You can also find Scott on Twitter @bedleybros or @TASFair_(tasfair.com).

Connected Classroom

It's been amazing to see the power of connection. The time of being limited to the four-walled area called a classroom is only by teacher decision now. My students have had the opportunity to connect and broaden their perspective through the relationships built with online video conferencing. Tools like Skype give the opportunity to learn about cultures and regions from those living there. Or they let us bring experts into our classrooms from around the globe. And it allows me to bring my students out into the world safely and with little cost and careful guidance. How would I suggest you get started? Here are the four steps to connecting your classroom to a world of learning.

Step 1: Start With the Learning

It's vital to start with your learning objective and work back from there. Many teachers stepping in to technology integration for the first time (beyond simple tools like word processing or presentations slides) will start with the tool and look to integrate that into their lessons. This isn't sustainable for a few reasons. First, tools are constantly changing and improving, so keeping up with the latest and greatest becomes the focus, rather than the learning, and it can be exhausting. It would be like starting your lesson planning with which type of pencil, pen, or crayon you want to use for the learning. Second, when you start with the tool, you may lose the core of the objective and focus more on learning the tool and how to use it. The kids can often figure out how to use the tools; it's our job as teachers to keep them focused on the learning outcomes. Finally, it can be intimidating having to feel like you know "everything" about technology. Let go of the notion of the teacher being the expert in all areas and embrace the role of facilitator of learning opportunities. Doing this models learning for your students.

If you start with the learning and use the tool to engage your students, it's exciting. You see those epiphanies in your target areas (or as we all know them "ah-ha" moments) happening for your students because of the high level of engagement in the learning. Stay focused on what it is you want your students to learn.

For example: In California, fifth graders are asked to learn about the 50 states and capitals of the United States. A teacher and class could just read about those, which is still a great way to learn. Or a teacher could first engage the students in a particular state by playing a game called Mystery Skype, where two classrooms from different states connect with each other online, without knowing where the other is located. They then use the process of elimination to discover where the other is located. The game is followed by an exchange between the students about their states. Even a short connection with a class from another state can be powerful, providing motivation for students to learn more through personal relationships with the class.

Step 2: Find the set-up that fits and don't do it alone.

No explorer really wants to go it alone, but they do want to go. Having a friend, a Personalized Learning Network, or a supportive IT department to help can be important. Which tool or community helps you connect the best with the tools or experiences that will help your students connect?

Step 3: Connect and Calendar

Using the latest communities like Skype in the classroom to connect with other teachers is great! These are simple to use, and you can find

(Continued)

(Continued)

like-minded educators. Be sure once you've set up your connection to get it on your calendar. Be sure not to forget tricky time zone conversions too.

Step 4: Reflect With Your Students

By far the reflection process from our connections to the world have been the most powerful. Take time to have your students talk to you and each other about why connecting to the world was important, what they learned, and how it changed their perspective. Those connections can go a long way toward developing empathy and global perspective.

Still want to learn more on how to connect? Check out Twitter and other forums for ways to learn to improve your craft of teaching. It is an awesome feeling to see your students so engaged!

Used with permission of Scott Bedley.

(Action Steps, continued)

with your personal and professional growth, or most importantly, the growth of your students. So, keep it simple:

A. Connect with a call, e-mail, Direct Tweet, Facebook post, and so on.

B. Establish a weekly or monthly meet-up (face-to-face, phone, or virtually).

C. Make sure to meet, even if it is just to check in and say hello.

2. Make a Decision

Keep in mind, your needs may differ from your students' needs. Making a connection for your own personal and professional growth may not always lead to connecting your classroom with another classroom. For example, you may decide that a teacher, who teaches a different grade level or subject, possesses the classroom management skills you admire. You decide to connect with her or him to bounce a few ideas or for accountability purposes. Let's say the two of you click, you begin to share some of your own effective strategies, and the relationship flourishes. This should not suggest that connecting your classrooms is the next logical step. In some instances, connecting locally or globally may be for the development of the teacher exclusively. To be certain you are making the right decision about connecting your classroom with another, take a moment and consider the following:

A. Will the current happenings in your classrooms enrich the learning of other students?

B. Do you understand the fundamental similarities and/or differences between your classroom and another?

C. Do you both feel confident about the available resources to support a successful connection/collaboration?

D. Are you both willing to commit the necessary time to connecting your classrooms?

3. Plan

Once you have established a consistent pattern of connecting with a peer educator, and you have decided to connect your classrooms, begin planning. The planning process will not be the same for everyone, and the outcome may be different as well. There is no written formula for what and how to plan, but it is necessary to plan for a successful connection/collaboration. There are four simple questions to answer, whether you are planning for a personal growth connection or a classroom connection:

A. What are your objectives?

B. What form of communication will you use?

C. How often and when will you meet?

D. What will be your measurable goal or final outcome?

4. Follow Through

Keep in mind that all classroom connections do not require elaborate plans. There are resources you may consider using, such as Mystery Skype or Quad Blogging (see the resources section on the Corwin Connected Educators companion website), that will connect your classroom for one day and extend the learning beyond the walls of your classroom. Either way you decide to go, remember to finish what you start.

Connecting to Build Your Classroom

Nicol R. Howard

What is the most effective strategy for preparing your classroom for the next academic year? As a new teacher, maybe you ask a former university professor for ideas. Or, maybe you consider the strategies of your former master teacher or mentor. Both approaches are a good start, but you don't want to forget about the potential needs of your students. Preparing a classroom involves much more than decorating walls, and it is no easy task. What would happen if you started with a blank slate? Do away with the premade posters or classroom decorations containing stereotypical colors and designs for your grade level. What are the implications for *students* making a contribution to the design of their classroom?

Although it is critical that you are aware of the role Common Core and technology are playing in the classroom, meeting your students' individual needs should come first. Student voice should direct your design path, so you will have to release the urge to have a ready-made classroom on the first day of school. Instead take the first day—make that the first weeks—of school getting to know your students through observations, questions, and even take-home questionnaires. You may just have to forget about the perfect rows of desks, as well as your neat corner desk and file cabinet. If you focused on designing your classroom to meet the recommendation of your district when implementing Common Core, you might have neat clusters of desks situated in groups of fours. Forgetting about mobile technology, you may have even planned to align desks on the wall near power outlets for desktop computers.

The introduction of Common Core, along with the advances in technology, has reshaped teaching and learning. Common Core strategies call for teachers to encourage collaborative conversations between students. If the desks were in neat rows, your students would have a clear view of the front of the classroom and/or the back of a classmate.

- Would you be comfortable if you were scheduled to meet a few friends at Starbucks and arrived to tables and chairs arranged in neat rows?
- How could you be expected to carry on a comfortable conversation with someone while twisting and turning in your seat, struggling to look him or her in the eye?
- And, how about the introduction of one-to-one devices?
- Could you imagine straight rows of desks with students heads buried in their own device?

The shift to collaborative conversations and the innovative use of technology in teaching and learning should challenge teachers to rethink classroom designs. At the same time, it is important to remember that the design of your classroom should not remain static. As students' needs change, so should their learning environment. Although the furniture supplied by your district is traditional, don't be afraid to take an unconventional approach to designing your own classroom. Take a risk!

If you decide that you will take a risk and go the untraditional route when designing your classroom, remember to make thoughtful and purposeful choices. In addition to connecting with a former professor or mentor for ideas, use your technology and lurk around on Instagram, Pinterest, and teacher blogs to collect ideas for your own classroom. Your classroom space should be comfortable and conducive for learning. Most importantly, keep in mind that what works for one teacher in their classroom may not work the same for you and your students in your own classroom. Visit the Corwin Connected Educators website for more resources related to this topic.

ACTION STEPS

1. Check It Out

Time may not allow for you to travel from school to school to see how other teachers organize and design their classrooms. Don't worry! There are enough teachers on social media that you can actually travel the world and peek into classrooms beyond your state border. Take the time to check out multiple teacher and classroom pages on all social media. You will likely discover a wealth of pictures and videos of classrooms, posted by teachers. Follow the teachers whose posts peak your curiosity, and remember that you don't necessarily have to reinvent the wheel. Check back periodically to see what's new in their room and watch for patterns in any changes they make, and carefully read any posts they make that may identify the reasons for changing the design of their classroom. For example:

A. Do the classrooms you see begin the year with seats in rows and later move to collaborative formations?

B. Do you notice that upper grade teachers begin and end with the same formations?

C. Do the classroom formations change seasonally, quarterly, or monthly?

(Action Steps continued on p. 30.)

PiP (Put It Into Practice) With Jamie Pesanti

Jamie Pesanti has her MA in teaching and learning in a global and diverse society. She is a veteran educator in the Santa Ana Unified School District. Jamie was nominated for teacher of the year in 2015. After teaching almost every grade level in K–5, she found her strengths lie in the upper grades where she can inspire a love of reading and rich dialogue around a wide range of genres. Her passion is working in a community where she can make a difference and truly connect with students and their families. She takes her students on a journey through the traveling stories and pictures she shares in her classroom. Jamie encourages each of her students to believe in themselves, to go to college, and to think outside the box.

By no means am I an expert on classroom environment, however, after 16 years of teaching in various elementary school classrooms, I have become very aware of how learning and work spaces affect our overall mood and productivity. This goes for teachers and students. An inviting, comfortable space is always more conducive to learning and teaching than a cold, generic environment. Let's face it—teachers are not wealthy, nor are we all artists. How can we create warm and inviting spaces in our classrooms without breaking the bank or spending countless hours on the weekends "designing" our classrooms? Here are four simple strategies that all teachers can use to create a space that wins the hearts and minds of our students, yet is cost effective and easy to create each year.

Look Around Your Room and Absorb Your Surroundings

- What do you see when you look around your classroom?
- What is on the walls? What colors do you see?
- What can you relate to?
- Does anything in the classroom bring you comfort?

When I set up my classroom each year, I use vivid colors that I enjoy looking at. Chances are, if the colors you are choosing are cheerful, your students will also notice and feel happier when they are sitting in there all day learning. I set up a corner of the room, or even use a door, at the beginning of the year to feature some my favorite things. I cover the section with my favorite colored paper and hang up pictures of my friends and family. I add a few pictures of my travels and even print out pictures of my favorite artists or drawings. I've even added pictures of my favorite healthy foods. Beginning the year by showing the students that I am a person with interests, just like them, allows them to see me as an individual and even brings them comfort. I am able to connect with students on a more personal level by doing this as well. Personal conversations ensure that I am able to share some of my life with students and ask about theirs. As the year goes on, you could even create a small space for students and choose a different student each week or every 2 weeks to bring in a few of their favorite pictures or items to put on display.

A Cozy Second Home

Students spend a large majority of time at school and in the classroom. Creating an environment that is warm and inviting makes a huge difference in the learning process. No one wants to go somewhere every day that is not a happy place to be. Each year, I make sure that I have divided different sections of my classroom into areas that are just for students. Every year, I bring in a rug (one that can be easily washed at home) and lay it in a corner of the room. I have bookshelves all around that area stocked with books that students can check out or read during class. These bookshelves have been bought at garage sales. I hang up my favorite posters about reading, travel, and adventure. Chinese lanterns hang up above the reading corner, and worn but cozy beanbags and beanbag chairs surround the rug. The students love this reading corner every year. The

(Continued)

(Continued)

table with the most points at the end of each day gets to read in the reading corner during the 25-minute silent reading period the next day and throughout the day whenever they have free time. Students who "think" they don't like to read are working very hard each day to get table points so that they can be the table reading in the reading corner. I make this area a very big deal, especially the first month of school. My students notice how much I love this area and treasure reading, and before you know it, they begin to treasure it as well.

A Print-Rich Environment Created by Students

My first year as a teacher, I spent hours and hours creating the "perfect classroom." The room was beautiful I thought and overwhelmingly print rich. I realized after a couple weeks that I didn't have any space, anywhere in the room to put up or display anything that belonged to the students. The room wasn't theirs; it was mine. It looked great in pictures, but it didn't belong to my students. It was my idea of what a classroom should look like, but they hardly noticed anything on the walls after the first day of school.

A classroom should be a space that is relevant and comforting to students. Creating spaces in the classroom where all student work is proudly hung and displayed helps students take ownership of their work and take pride in what they are learning. I have one science board where our latest projects, experiments, and investigations are hung or stapled. I have string hanging from the lights above each table where their latest art projects are displayed above their tables. The Language Arts Board is an interactive space where character trait posters, drawings from our novels, Venn diagrams, questions and answers, or connections to other texts that students have made, and so on, can be taped up by them or me. This year, a student excitedly waited for me at the door before school. She was waiting to show me the clear plastic bag she had brought to hang up on the Language

Arts Board. In it was a rattle from a rattlesnake that her uncle had given her. The day before, we had read about a rattlesnake in the novel *Holes,* and she wanted to share her connection with the class. The class was thrilled and all got to go up to the board to touch and feel the rattle. More students began bringing in things to hang up on the board—things that were meaningful to them and relevant to what we were learning.

There are more boards in my classrooms for math, social studies, poetry, and writing. I realized that I only needed to have these areas set up at the beginning of the year, ready for student work. I explained during the first week of school that once we were proud of something we have worked on, it would be displayed and hung in the appropriate areas of the class. When students have a few moments of free time, they can "walk the room" and see their own work displayed or the work of their peers. They can read each other's final drafts or see different perspectives of the same paintings or poetry that they themselves also have on display. The classroom becomes much more meaningful when it belongs to the students and when they know where to find their best work.

Pinterest

By creating your own free boards on Pinterest, you can explore and browse to get plenty of options on how to set up your classroom. Not only can you search for any idea you can possibly imagine, but also you can "pin" anyone's idea to your board and save it for future reference. There are ideas on Pinterest for activities in every subject, but I like to use it to give me ideas on ways to set up my classroom. Sharing and exploring on Pinterest can help you feel inspired in your classroom each year. Empowering ourselves is an important concept in education. By empowering students in the classroom and allowing them to take ownership of the environment, teachers and students will experience a more pleasant daily experience.

Used with permission of Jamie Pesanti.

2. Ask Questions

Since every classroom is different, it may be important for you go a step further than lurking or following teachers on social media before adopting their ideas. Consider posting a few questions for the teachers you follow, such as:

A. How many students do you have in your classroom?

B. If you could change one thing about your classroom, what would that be?

C. What do your students enjoy most about your classroom design?

3. Remain Flexible

As mentioned earlier in this chapter, every classroom is different. Your students are different, you are a different teacher than your colleague, and your location may be different. After checking out multiple classroom environments, remain flexible and open to accept that adjustments may be necessary. In some instances, you may be able to prepare for the "unexpected"; however, there may come a time when a complete overhaul is required. One example of an "unexpected" occurrence may be a new student added to the roster. Adding a new student may lead to reconfiguring the desks or tables in your room. Here are a few more situations that may call for flexibility in your classroom design:

A. Your students ask if they can redesign the classroom, because they want it to reflect the current topic you are studying.

B. A student no longer cooperates well with his or her collaborative group, and you realize that it may be time to switch things up a bit.

C. You observe one group always on task and another struggling to focus, so you move a few students to new tables.

D. Your new unit of study requires students to sit and listen to you longer than usual, so you make room on the carpet for beanbags and pillows.

4. Observe Your Students

Since the needs of every student differs, it is important to observe your students to assess their needs. We know students are good at giving verbal and nonverbal cues when expressing their feelings about their surroundings. Watch for the frowns and smiles when you change the design of your classroom. For example, a student who typically enjoys dim lights in the room may not be getting enough sleep at night. Now the dim lights he or she once enjoyed put him or her to sleep. Or, your neat and tidy student begins compulsively asking if you need help cleaning the classroom at the end of the day. Appropriate lighting and minimal clutter are simple things to consider; however, the bigger issue is related to the immediate needs of your students. In order to make sure that your students are comfortable and cozy in the classroom, simply observe and respond to their needs.

5. Include to Engage

In order to engage and become prepared for academic success, students must be given opportunities to take ownership of their learning. The action of taking ownership reflects the notion of student agency. Student agency is about engaging your students in every aspect of their learning process, including the design of their room. If you are teaching upper elementary or secondary, including your students in the process of building their dream classroom will certainly contribute to the ownership of and engagement in their learning.

Making Connections for Planning Your Teaching

Lisa Dabbs

A *lesson plan* is a teacher's detailed guide or map. It maps the course of instruction for one class, or maybe many if you teach more than one subject. It's the *recipe* for the day's exciting learning!

A daily or weekly lesson plan is developed by a teacher to guide class instruction. Details will vary depending on the preference of the teacher and the subject matter being covered. Schools or school districts may have guidelines regarding the lesson plan. They may even have mandates.

That being said, there's always a way to make your lesson plan uniquely your own. How to prepare the lesson plan will also be important. Some teachers enjoy using a good sturdy lesson plan book, some a Word document or spreadsheet, or still others a shared Google document (Google Doc). Whichever way you choose, the need for a lesson plan is vital. It can be even more challenging to write and prepare a lesson plan when you're a new teacher!

Without a detailed plan, your lesson will be lacking the key components to make it meaningful. A poorly planned lesson is not something you want to be in the habit of designing. Students are the ones who will suffer when we fail to appropriately plan for them.

As you get ready to plan your lesson, it encompasses a lot more than a textbook, curriculum maps, or standards. These resources are important, and you should use them—but they should be seen as guides to lesson development. For me it comes down to being able to meet your students where they are and develop lessons that support their needs. Let this knowledge drive your planning. Creating lessons that are based only on district standards, or what should get done, will result in big gaps in the learning. Consider planning your lessons using a backwards-mapping approach. Look at the whole year, and map backwards from the end of the school year forward. This may seem challenging, but it's helpful to start with the end results that you know will be expected for your students and grade level.

Data is an important consideration as a lesson is developed but can be scary for a new teacher. Take a deep breath and keep in mind that you are collecting data daily as you talk to your students, observe them, see their successes and also where they need support. Data can come in lots of forms such as a quiz, question, or exit slip. Use the information you derive from these tools to meet your students where they are, find gaps in their learning, and make that the guiding force in your teaching and lesson plan.

> For lesson planning, start with the end results that you know will be expected for your students and grade level.

PiP (Put It Into Practice) With Layla Wiedrick Henry

Layla Henry, M.Ed., is an educational blogger and teacher who always seeks to engage her students by creating accessible yet rigorous lessons. From the beginning, she has worked to produce an engaging classroom environment for her students, especially English Language Learners, through technology and creativity. Over the past 8 years, she has worked at a diverse range of schools within her district but has always found a way to actively contribute to her grade-level team. She was nominated for teacher of the year in 2013. Her blog, www.fancy freein4th.com touches on topics such as classroom management and student engagement.

Teacher Connectedness: Beyond Four Walls

Remember the feeling that you had at the end of your credential program? You got your feet wet student teaching and were ready to take on a class all your own. As good as my credential program was, over my 8 years of teaching, I have come to realize that there are so many things that teachers have to learn in the classroom. When I entered my first year of teaching, I was eager to put all of the theory I had learned into practice. However, my first years of teaching were filled with unforeseen transitions that made it difficult to plant my roots and grow. For example:

- How do I integrate into a preexisting grade-level team?

- How do I be a young teacher with lots of ideas and not annoy veteran teachers?

- How do I cope with being displaced . . . again?

- How do I switch grade levels gracefully?

- How do I connect with teachers, build relationships with school communities, and hone in on my craft when I've been shuffled around?

(Continued)

(Continued)

I started teaching at a time when there wasn't a lot of stability for novice teachers due to a variety of factors. Classrooms closed and teachers were shuffled around to new schools and grade levels. After my second year of teaching, I was one of many new teachers laid off because of a reduction in force. I had given up hope of being called back the next year, and when late August rolled around, I felt disheartened. However, my phone rang the Sunday after school had begun, and the district offered me a job teaching sixth and seventh grade. Moving up to the intermediate level was nerve wracking to say the least, but I knew this would be my only opportunity to get my foot back in the door.

I took a blind leap of faith into middle school regardless of the fact that I would be starting back at square one. I had to navigate new curriculum, school culture, and staff relationships, and then try to figure out how I fit into all of this. I had never in my wildest dreams expected to teach ancient civilizations and mythology. I was completely overwhelmed, and that is when I stumbled upon http://www.teachers payteachers.com (TpT). To say TpT was a godsend to me during that year of teaching would be an understatement. I was able to get a grasp on how to teach these foreign standards in practical but inventive ways. TpT exposed me to creative teachers who had developed rigorous materials to supplement their curriculum. These lessons inspired me, supported me, and helped me through the year.

I got word of a 4/5 combination class opening for the following year and said farewell to intermediate school and hello to a classroom ranging from 8- to 12-year-olds. All summer, I spent hours scouring Pinterest for organizational strategies and curriculum management ideas that catered to a combo class. It was here that I found links to

You may be tempted to plan lessons alone, but don't. Collaborating to design lessons will be more powerful in the long run. Encourage your school's grade-level team to meet, share ideas, and plan. If that's not an option, find at least one trusted colleague, carve out some time, share resources, and plan. This is also where the teacher blogs, and eventually, with the help of one of my best friends, Michelle Griffo from Apples and ABC's, I started my own blog, Fancy Free in 4th. I began to engage in the ongoing conversations surrounding education, and I began to network and connect with passionate and dedicated teachers. I have continued to nurture these online friendships through Instagram as well. For me, it's a quick way to visually share what is going on in my classroom, ask questions, or highlight different products or books that are working for my students.

These online communities have led to blogger meet-ups where we get together in person and chat about the changes in education, how they have adapted their curriculum, and memorable classroom stories. I was encouraged to start my own TpT store to share what has worked for me in my classroom. Having other teachers encourage me to share my ideas and express interest in curriculum that I developed validated and encouraged me. These meet-ups led to invitations into a variety of teacher Facebook groups where I have connected with hundreds of other teachers by grade level and region. Inside of these forums, we ask practical teaching questions and share resources to help support our classrooms and build lesson plans.

These social networks combined have given me immeasurable support as I have navigated the past 8 years in a profession that is constantly changing. Engaging and participating in these virtual communities where teachers from across the world share resources and ideas, and offer professional and personal support has challenged me and made me feel a sense of connectedness that I was lacking. As a result of all of this, I feel a connectedness to a staff regardless of where I teach.

Used with permission of Layla Wiedrick Henry.

development of a social media community is key. By reaching out, say on Twitter or Google Plus, you'll find that there are educators all too ready to help and provide resources, and maybe even share a lesson or two. Visit www.corwin.com/connectededucators for more resources on this topic.

ACTION STEPS

1. Set Your Lesson Objective

A. As easy as this may sound, your objective is what you want the outcome of the lesson to be. This is what you want the students to know and be able to do at the end of the lesson. You may want to do a "backwards mapping" exercise as you prepare the lesson.

B. If you are unsure about your objective, consider connecting to a mentor or online Personalized Learning Network social media contact and ask them for feedback.

C. As you develop your objectives, let your students be your guides.

D. Consider your school or district's guidelines, textbooks, and standards as you work on setting objectives.

2. List/Organize Your Lesson Materials

A. Your materials are the list of resources, articles or manipulatives you need. This helps you organize everything prior to the lesson.

B. Think the lesson all the way through. Do you need to place an order with your school's secretary? Will you need to plan your own purchases? Can you recycle some items from home? You need to have all your materials complete as you prepare your plan.

C. Will your materials include technology hardware or applications? Will students or parents be bringing in supplies? These are important questions to ask as you plan.

3. Define Your Lesson Procedures

A. Consider activation of students' prior knowledge. What will that look like in your lesson? Will you start with a video, poem, song, or story?

B. Teaching and learning activities will be part of this process. What are the steps you will take as you present and guide this lesson? Scripting these out ahead of time may give a level of confidence to your lesson that is needed as you start.

C. What questions will you use to guide student thought? There may be some options available to you via your school's textbooks or those you've developed with colleagues.

4. Have a Lesson Assessment

A. How will you know that your students "got it"? Consider using various ways to gather assessment data for your lesson.

B. Assessment happens throughout the lesson. As you are going through the process make notes—even mental ones—about how it's going.

C. As the lesson comes to a close, you will need to check for understanding to see if objectives were met. How will you accomplish this task? What tool or tools will you have in place to gather feedback from your students? There are great tools such as Evernote, which will allow you to record feedback from the lesson.

D. Consider using an exit slip to document learning. Have students write their responses on a 3 x 5 card. Examples: "Write one thing you learned today," "I would like to learn more about . . .".

E. Review your assessment tool (e.g., an exit slip) to determine how you may need to adjust your instruction to better meet the needs of your students.

5. Reflect on the Lesson

A. Making time to reflect on lessons taught is critical. A successful teacher is the one who takes time to consistently evaluate and reevaluate his or her pedagogy. Consider using a journal as a way to write down thoughts about successful outcomes as well as areas that need improvement.

B. Set up a Google Doc where you consistently record your ideas on lesson plan performance.

C. Using social media tools such as a blog to document reflections on lessons is a great way to connect with others who could provide supportive feedback by way of comments on your post.

D. Use video to record your insights regarding the points of your lessons that you find successful and what needs improvement.

E. Tech tools like Evernote provide a resource where written as well as recorded notes can be kept regarding lesson reflective process.

Making Connections to Communicate With Students and Parents

Lisa Dabbs and Nicol R. Howard

By now, you are well aware that schools are like a home-away-from-home for students. Some students wake up in the morning excited to come to school, and others can't wait to return home. No matter which student you actually have in your classroom, it is important to create a sense of community for them and their families. Creating a sense of community encourages students to become more engaged in the learnings of their class. Parents volunteer more often and support however they can when they know what is going on in their child's class. In the past, it was as simple as sending home a weekly written or typed letter about the current classroom happenings. We were doing something big when we started sending home newsletters created in Microsoft publisher. Now, more than ever, communication between school and home can no longer travel one way. Considering the need to support second-language learners in many of our schools, mastering the art of communication with our diverse populations is also key. Monologues have faded, and the dialogues between schools and homes are more desirable and effective.

As a result of technological changes, building and maintaining a classroom community has become simpler in some regards. You can invite your students and their families to be a part of the community through the use of Web-based resources such as Edmodo, blogs, Wikispaces, Volunteerspot, Remind (formerly Remind 101), and various Google features. Parents may also opt-in to the use of Twitter as a tool to keep up with classroom happenings or to connect with questions. The complex issues related to connecting to communicate with students are access and digital citizenship. Although access to technology at home and at low-socioeconomic schools raises a broader concern that we do not address in this chapter, digital citizenship is one lesson that can be learned through classroom activities. We hope to provide you with rich examples of technology used to communicate with students and parents, as well as practical ideas for supporting your students as they become digital citizens. You'll find more resources on this topic at www.corwin.com/connectededucators.

Lisa: As I began to connect with teachers through New Teacher Chat #ntchat on Twitter, it became apparent that new teachers were really struggling with how to connect to parents. Their lack of experience in just how to get those connections started was shared in numerous chat conversations. Inevitably the issue of waiting until the last minute, when a student in their class had become disruptive and contact with a parent had to be made, became problematic. Making first contact with a parent over a student discipline matter is not the best way to begin to build trust. Through many #ntchat conversations around the importance of connecting to parents from the beginning of school, resources were shared to guide this work. One of the most successful ways for connecting early to parents and sharing the "good news" about students is to use a tool that will support collaboration such as Remind at https://www.remind.com/. Remind can be used on your smartphone, laptop, or tablet device. It provides a way to reach out to parents and students via text, images, and voice without sharing your cell number directly. By learning to utilize a simple tool such as Remind, you are facilitating important parent-teacher communication, conversation, and collaboration about your classroom and student activities in a way that is fresh and engaging.

Nicol: I will never forget the day when my first parent followed me on Twitter. I thought, "What do I do? Should I follow back?" I did. This hard-working mother navigated her 40-hour work week like clockwork, and rarely missed a beat. Nearly 2 weeks after following me, I heard from her by direct message (DM) on Twitter. She wanted to know if she could change the time of our parent-teacher conference to an earlier time slot. I was happy to oblige, but I was even happier that she found an efficient and effective way to reach me. I heard from her several more times over the course of the year. On one occasion she asked a question about homework, which led into a back-and-forth DM of pictures and homework help links to supplement what she was working on at home with her child. Toward the end of the year, I actually sent her a DM asking if her child would be able to attend a summer STEM (Science, Technology, Engineering, and Mathematics) program. Another time she sent me a simple thank you for doing what I love—teaching. I can only imagine the peace of mind that comes along with an increased level of access to teachers. Although Twitter worked for me, it may not work for your communication purposes. You may prefer to keep your lines of communication open during school hours only. If so, consider how you will reach and stay connected to working parents who desire to be engaged and connected with the teaching and learning of their child.

PiP (Put It Into Practice) With Bill Selak

Bill Selak is the director of technology at Hillbrook School in Silicon Valley, and adjunct faculty member at Azusa Pacific University. He is an ISTE 2014 Kay L. Bitter Vision Award recipient, ISTE 2013 Emerging Leader, Google Certified Teacher, and he served on the California State Superintendent's Education Technology Task Force. Bill has been on the planning teams of EdCampSFBay and EdCampLA. Bill has presented on music in the classroom, taking risks in education, visual literacy, video in the classroom, flipped classrooms, online professional development, publishing with iBooks, and photography in the classroom. See #eduawesome and http://www.billselak.com.

Connecting with parents is everything. If you can communicate what your students are doing in a timely, effective way, parents will love you. Technology makes it very easy to connect with parents. Here are three of my favorite tools.

Remind.com

Remind is "a safe way for teachers to text message students and stay in touch with parents." As a second-grade teacher, I used Remind to share projects, resources, videos, and reminders with parents.

My favorite example of using Remind is from our field trip to the Natural History Museum. In primary grades, field trips are a huge deal. Most parents want to chaperone; all parents want to participate in some way. During the field trip, I shared photos with parents via Remind. Parents saw their child on the bus, in Exposition Park in downtown Los Angeles, and gigantic dinosaur fossils. This wasn't the best part, though. By far, the coolest part of the day was when I used Animoto to create a slideshow while we were driving back to school. Before we left Downtown, I shared, "Here's a slideshow of our field trip

today: http://animoto.com/play/x1xK0Py110ZlYoipuTUisg." By the time
we got off the bus, most parents had watched the video. While
students were getting picked up, conversations were *not,* "How was
the field trip?" Instead, I heard things like "That woolly mammoth was
huge!" and "That statue was amazing!"

YouTube Videos

Another way I connected my classroom with parents was through a
daily recap video. I recorded a YouTube video for parents giving a quick
overview of the learning that happened that day. It was unedited, and
always one-take, so that it was sustainable. I shared the videos with
parents via Remind and on my class website. YouTube makes it so easy
to record and upload videos these days. If you haven't considered
recording one-take videos for your students, parents, or community, I
highly recommend it.

A Class Website

The final significant way that I communicated with parents was through
my class website. I've taught several grades, so I've had several sites, but
my favorite is k5tunes.com. This site was for my fourth- and fifth-grade
music students and parents. It had announcements, resources, and most
notably, instrument tutorials (http://k5tunes.com/instruments). A fellow
music teacher, Sharon Cathey, and I created several tutorials for beginning
players of the flute, clarinet, trumpet, trombone, and saxophone. (You
want some entertainment? Watch me play the trombone!) Despite only
teaching these band students one hour per week in person, the website
enabled me to teach 24/7 to my budding musicians. They could play
along with us, or just listen. Whatever their method, this class website
allowed me to connect with parents anytime and anywhere.

Used with permission of Bill Selak.

ACTION STEPS

1. Begin on a Positive Note

Always give attention to the positives and start this process early! There are far too many good reasons for establishing communication between students and parents using technology. If too much time is spent on addressing the reasons why you shouldn't connect (using social media or Web-based tools) for communication, reframe the dialogue to address all of the positives. Introduce this form of communication in a positive manner by highlighting the benefits of connecting to communicate using Web-based tools and/or social media, such as:

A. This form of communication reduces the response time between you and your students and/or parents.

B. Learning to communicate in this fashion teaches your students how to be digital citizens in a real-world context.

C. You can potentially avoid misunderstandings down the road by building trust right at the beginning via early positive communication.

2. Seek the Best Communication Method

E-mail may be your first go-to means of communication with parents, but remember that there are other ways to communicate using technology. Through the use of social media tools such as Twitter, Facebook, Google Plus, and blogs you can establish ways for sharing classroom learning and events that is vibrant and often in real time. Using a tool such as Remind will allow for frequent classroom updates. How you communicate with parents may not be the form of communication you choose to use with your students. You must also consider the grade level you teach. For example, you wouldn't expect your fourth graders to DM you on Twitter with a homework question. Nor would you expect your fifth-grade students to get a cell phone alert when you post a message on Edmodo. But setting up a public or private Facebook community for your class adds a layer of open dialogue that most parents will welcome.

A. Think about your purpose for communicating and establish the tool that you think will connect best for that purpose.

B. More than likely you will communicate with parents if your students are in the primary grades, so think about the tools your parents can use. Consider your grade-level and take a quick poll at back-to-school night to determine which tool will work best.

C. Establish a Twitter account for your class and encourage students to tweet and have parents check in for updates. (This may be preferable to using your personal one.)

D. Set up a private or public Facebook or Google Plus page for your class that parents can use to participate in as well as to keep in touch with ongoing activities.

E. Start a class blog as a way to keep in touch with parents and share the learning in your classroom. Linda Yollis in California is an amazing example of how that can work. Use her resources and adapt it to your grade level.

F. Establish a Remind account for your class. All you need to get started is a willingness to use the tool. It will be transformational.

3. Invite Parents In

Parents are our students' first teachers. We hear this often, but frequently don't know how to capitalize on this strength. Our parents will come to us with a variety of skill sets and that's the key to finding ways to draw on their experience to add richness to your classroom. You may be tempted to set up a traditional "room parent" model, and that's fine, but also think outside the box!

A. Think about the needs that you will have in your classroom based on a yearly plan. Consider emailing a tool such as a Google Form to gather parent information. Backwards map to each month or quarterly theme. See where the talents that your parents have can fit into that framework.

B. Set up opportunities for parents to volunteer to support your students in classroom activities, out-of-class material development, and with potential field trips. Don't forget to draw in the working parent who has a desire to help but may not be able to be there physically in the classroom.

C. Establish some evening curriculum activities and ask parents and students to help set up and run Parent Nights. Choose events that students and parents can easily collaborate on together. Seek out those parents whose skills match well to the content. Reading, Math, and Science Nights are always fun, but how about a Maker Night, Book Making Night, Author Night, Poetry Slam Night, Tech Tool, or App Smashing Night too! Set aside time in class for students to help you develop and plan these parent nights to make it a real collaboration.

D. Have a Google Hangout Night! Invite parents and students to plan their event and then use Google to live-stream it to those who might not be able to be present.

E. Parents may have language needs. Be sure to plan to have a colleague or older student available to translate for the event so that no parent feels left out of the classroom activity.

Connecting to a Mentor: Virtual and Collaborative

Lisa Dabbs

Mentoring matters. It matters, because it offers acceptance, guidance, instructional support, hope, and optimism to teachers—particularly to new teachers. The act of mentoring is a part of the fabric of many educational institutions. Yet it's still a piece that's missing at our schools for those new to the education profession.

Mentors are an important part of the process of a new teacher's career. A good mentor can offer just the right kind of insight, support and guidance to set a new teacher on the right path in their practice. A mentor should serve as the "guide on the side" as a new teacher is developing their craft. This guide that comes alongside a new teacher can be just the thing that makes the difference between a new teacher who is thriving or one who is merely surviving.

Connecting an experienced teacher to one new to the practice can be a challenge. Often those veteran staff at a school site may lack the desire to mentor or at times the skill set to provide a new colleague the support they need. However, the opportunities to collaborate with a potential "virtual" mentor via social media or other online community are limitless. These virtual mentors can fill the gap with much needed feedback and support where a face-to-face mentor may not be available. Seeking a mentor, whether they be teaching next door or across the state, is an action that can ultimately lead to a very meaningful collaboration.

LOSING HOPE

In my early blogging journey, I began to explore the notion of mentoring. I reflected on my work as an educator, trying to recall the people in my past who had mentored me and those I had mentored. While doing this, I came up with an acronym for my consultant practice that I call IMET: Inspire, Mentor, and Equip Teachers (to teach with soul). It summed up for me what I believe a true mentor does. Unfortunately, with the current challenges we face in education, I recognize it's hard for educators to take the time to truly IMET.

About 2 years ago, I landed on the blog of a new teacher. One of her recent posts was titled "Losing Hope." The teacher started the post by saying that she had a dream: a dream to be the best teacher she could be, to be the kind of teacher that students would be inspired by. Unfortunately, there were no clear expectations set for this teacher at her school—and worse, no support. This teacher's perception was that they would be supported as first-year teachers. Instead they were placed in a "sink-or-swim" position. So this teacher sank.

MY RESPONSE

I was moved by this teacher's post, and I responded. Here's some of what I shared with this young teacher who asked for "positive and encouraging words":

When I read your words, "I believe I was under the illusion that I had support and help from all angles, when in reality, I hadn't felt more alone and lost," my heart went out to you. I was an elementary school principal for 14 years. During those years I consistently spent time mentoring, supporting, and guiding my teachers. It's truly my passion. If you read the research on why young people like yourself leave the teaching profession, it turns out that it is exactly for those reasons you describe. A school should work to foster a culture where its teachers collaborate and learn from one another. This is at the heart of how educators grow as professionals. Some of my colleagues still struggle with this piece. I apologize. We need to do much better.

I entered the teaching profession in my early twenties as a kindergarten teacher. I was fortunate to come from a family of educators. However, I still encountered a great deal of frustration and anxiety in my first year. I felt very alone, as I did not have a supportive principal, or mentor. I was new to the school. My kinder team members believed in "kill and drill" for kindergarten kids and I was mortified! In addition to that, no one on staff had a child development degree. As a result they weren't pleased when I began to talk about child development issues and how those directly influenced how children learn and should be allowed to develop. The use of hands-on learning opportunities vs. paper-pencil tasks was not well received. The bottom line is that my first few years were rough! Did I have a mentor teacher? No. Was it hard? Extremely. But I kept pressing forward because I believed in myself and cared deeply for my students.

MENTORS OFFER HOPE

As I finished my response, I was frustrated at the idea of the lack of mentoring support we are providing, even now, to those new to the profession. I was frustrated with the fact that this enthusiastic new teacher fell and no one was there to come alongside and lift her up. Why did this teacher lose hope? We know so much more now about how to retain and support new teachers. So where was her mentor? No new teacher should have to stick it out alone. A mentor can provide the help—and hope—that can turn the tide of a difficult situation for a new teacher.

I believe strongly in the power of mentoring. I believe that this relationship is vital to the success of a new teacher. However, not all experienced teachers at a school site are able to take on this challenge. Over 2 years ago, I had the idea that if there weren't enough experienced teachers at a school site who could, or were willing to mentor a new teacher, why not a virtual mentor who would be willing to lend support? As a result the Teacher Mentoring Project was born! If you're a new teacher or an experienced teacher who could benefit from a mentoring relationship, I urge you to seek out this group on LisaDabbs.com/new-teacher-mentoring -project. To date, 156 educators from around the globe have made themselves available to mentor virtually, through the first years and beyond

Why aren't we making the time to mentor? Is it too challenging? Too much work? With the availability of Web 2.0 and social media tools, mentors could easily collaborate with a new teacher and offer a wealth of supportive online resources such as education websites, lesson plans, blogs, wikis, Twitter, and e-books. The power of these tools to support and mentor new teachers has great potential in the 21st century teaching model. With that said, I hope that in spite of the issues we face each day, you'll consider reaching out to find a mentor or support a new teacher and be a mentor. I believe that by connecting to a mentor—either on your site, at your school, or via a virtual process—can make the difference

PiP (Put It Into Practice) With Betina Hsieh

Dr. Betina Hsieh is an assistant professor of teacher education at California State University, Long Beach. Her teacher education work is informed by 10 years of urban middle school classroom experience, literacy coaching, and work as codirector of the Bay Area Writing Project. Current research interests include coteaching, the emergence and development of a teacher professional identity, the development of cross-content literacy practices (particularly in the age of the Common Core Standards), and the development and uses of 21st century literacy practices in schools and universities. You can follow Betina on Twitter @Profhsieh.

Sharing Resources, Experiences, and Journeys: A Philosophy of Mentoring

Although I've grown and changed a lot as a teacher throughout the years, my core philosophy toward collaborative mentorship has remained the same: share resources, share experiences, and share journeys.

Sharing Resources

There are some that believe in the "sink-or-swim" method of mentoring in which mentors just provide space and mentees must figure out how to teach on their own within a "safe space" of the mentor's classroom. This is pretty much the opposite of how I operate. In my mentoring philosophy, I value sharing as many resources as possible with those I'm mentoring. For new and continuing teachers, this means sharing resources by modeling in my teacher education classes but also via multiple methods on the Internet. My professional Twitter account (https://twitter.com/ProfHsieh) and several boards on my Pinterest account (https://www.pinterest.com/betinahsieh/) are dedicated to sharing and collecting resources for teachers. I really appreciate the way that social media has allowed me to continue sharing resources

(Continued)

(Continued)

with my credential candidates long after they leave my classroom and establish their own.

Sharing Experiences

One of the central beliefs that I've always had about teaching and mentoring at any level is that students don't come in as empty vessels, devoid of their own contributions and experiences. In mentoring teachers that are newer to the profession, I find this to be especially true. The credential candidates and new teachers that I've worked with have a plethora of important experiences in and out of classrooms that they draw from to form their ideas of teaching and learning, just as I have a variety of sources and experiences from which I draw mine. An important aspect of my mentoring work is that we share these experiences as well as reflecting on the shared experiences we create throughout our time together. This allows newer teachers to openly discuss positive and negative experiences with schools as well as some of their professional experiences related to their content areas or their work with youth. We do this, again both through in-class activities and through sharing on virtual discussion board forums and through Twitter chats. Through sharing these experiences, we grow and learn together.

Sharing Journeys

This leads me to the final key component of my mentoring work, which is sharing the journey with my students. To me, sharing the journey means that I walk the path alongside the teachers I am mentoring. I keep myself open to learning. I engage in our online and in-person discussions. I reflect on my own journey through maintaining this professional blog. And, I ask students to do the same through constant reflection, engagement in online and in-person discussions, and being open to new ideas. By walking together and being authentic about the victories, hard-fought or simple, and challenges of our work, we avoid the isolation that drives so many people away from our important work.

Used with permission of Betina Hsieh.

in how successful you are in your practice. Drop by www.corwin .com/connectededucators for additional supportive resources.

What can we do every day as educators to provide mentoring support?

ACTION STEPS

1. Reach Out and Connect to a Virtual Mentor

Start your journey to become part of the New Teacher Mentoring Project by going to www.lisadabbs.com/new-teacher-mentoring -project. The steps to connect to a virtual mentor or to sign up to become a mentor aren't challenging.

To become a mentor:

1. If you are a teacher looking to mentor another, please fill out the form in #2 below.
2. Info Sheet for Mentor Program: for interested mentors go to http://goo.gl/6hEXZp.
3. Fill out all the information as shown in the example on the Google Doc.
4. Your info will then be placed on a public-view-only doc by Lisa Dabbs.
5. Look to be contacted to become a mentor to a new or preservice teacher.

To find a mentor:

1. Search this Google Doc Mentor Information sheet (view only) at http://goo.gl/rQR4j1.
2. Find an educator on the Google Doc and e-mail him or her through the information he or she has provided to connect for mentoring support.
3. You are more than welcome to have more than one mentor!
4. Join the New Teacher Google Community at http://bit.ly/ntch atgoogleplus and/or New Teacher Chat Facebook Community at https://www.facebook.com/NewTeacherChat. Check in weekly to talk, exchange experiences, and seek out resources.

2. The New Teacher Mentoring Project Purpose

- To collaborate and find best practices
- To mentor and support new/preservice teachers in K–12 and higher education institutes of learning worldwide for online and offline learning.
- To use the New Teacher Mentoring project to help new teachers navigate through your first few years of teaching with a virtual mentor.

We trust that you will find these action steps useful in the process of working with and connecting to a mentor, locally or globally, who can come alongside you in your practice. We also hope that you will be encouraged to reach out and join the New Teacher Mentoring Project outlined in the Action Steps above.

BE ENCOURAGED TO GET CONNECTED

The opportunities to be empowered and connected in the real world, as well as the virtual world, are endless. There are many inspiring educators who want to see you succeed and are eager to support you, and it starts with reaching out and seeking those opportunities. We hope to continue standing in the gap to support you as you move to the next level and encourage you to stay connected.

A SAGE Company

Helping educators make the greatest impact

CORWIN HAS ONE MISSION: to enhance education through intentional professional learning.

We build long-term relationships with our authors, educators, clients, and associations who partner with us to develop and continuously improve the best evidence-based practices that establish and support lifelong learning.

Solutions you want. Experts you trust. Results you need.